THE GAME

THE GAME

10
Part Series

SHAKILA KENDALL
Shardell Martin

THE GAME
(10 PART SERIES)

Author: Shakila Martin-Kendall
Cover Design: Shardell Martin

Self Published

The Game (10 Part Series)
ISBN: 979-8-9859761-0-6
E-Book: 979-8-9859761-1-3

DEDICATION

This series is dedicated to all those who loss a loved one to gun violence and those who are ready for CHANGE!!!

My prayer is that the Holy Spirit comforts you in the midst of your grief and creates change that takes place in the heart and teaches you to grieve in a healthy way I pray that God will restore the family dynamic back to our communities and instill values and morals in the people Father God in the name of Jesus move by your spirit because we need You like never before to move on behalf of our neighborhoods we need you to pour out your Love and teach us how to Love one another as you Love us Lord God we need you to remove the wickedness from our hearts and the mentality of hate and create an epidemic of LOVE AND COMPASSION AND FORGIVENESS I pray God that you have mercy upon us all and draw us closer to you through every trial and obstacle that we face I pray that we remember that you are still God in every situation so God shift our minds and our perceptions of who you are and create new mindsets, new perspectives on life, and new lifestyles for your people In Jesus name I pray Amen!

2 CHRONICLES 7:14

If my people, which are called by my name, shall humble themselves, and pray, and seek my face, and turn from their wicked ways; then will I hear from heaven, and will forgive their sin, and will heal their land

FOREWORD

. On December 2nd, 2018 I received a phone call that would change my family forever. As we all know death of a loved one can be a hard thing to accept but there is a different type of pain present when a loved one life is taken from them. I remember being in the midst of tending to my children when my sister called and said my cousin was shot and instantly, I felt my heart drop but I shifted my mind and thought ok shot doesn't have to mean he is gone. My family quickly gathered at the hospital. We cried and prayed and cried and prayed some more and finally at 10:06 p.m. Tashon Martin was pronounced dead and then it happened. I released a scream that I had never released before, I felt a pain that I had never felt before. I later came to realize that the scream was not just for my pain and grief but it was for his wife, daughter, my family, you and anyone else who have experienced this type of loss to gun violence. I received a word in the midst of my anguish concerning purpose and it never left me. I decided to write a poem for my cousin's funeral and the response from the people sparked something else in me. After having a conversation with my sister, who mentioned the word series, that was all God needed me to hear to birth this series. Too many of us have experienced this pain and desire to see change. I knew God wanted to use me to bring change in my community but didn't expect it to be in this format. I knew it was time for me to be the change I want to see. I encourage everyone who is reading this to have an open mind and allow God to speak to you. I want those who loss a loved one to violence to be encouraged and comforted and to know that I see and carry your burden with you. I want those who are in the streets to know that God loves you no matter what you have done and it is never too late for change and to walk in the purpose that God has for you!!!

ACKNOWLEDGEMENTS

Special Thanks to My:
Husband- for supporting me through this journey, being my life partner, not allowing me to give up when discouraged and just for sticking with me through the good and the bad

Sister/Pastor- for speaking a word that birthed the idea of a series, for always inspiring me even when you don't know it and always pushing me to strive for greatness/excellence...I don't know where I would be in life without God constantly using you to impart into me

Aunt Wanda and Cousin Nakia- for brainstorming subtitles with me

Aunt Kim -for speaking what God gave you concerning my purpose and gun violence

Mom- for being a listening ear and helping me develop in different areas of my life

Father- for always being positive and encouraging me to continue on the right path

Grandmothers- for helping raise me to never give up no matter how difficult life gets

God sister-for sharing your wisdom and insight

Prophetess Mary- for support and encouragement through creativity process

Tashon Martin- for being who you were and having such a huge impact on this family.... you are forever embedded in our hearts

God- saved the best for last, I give honor to You who birthed these poems out of me in only 3 sittings...I could not believe the wisdom You were imparting in me so quickly...Thank you Jesus because without You there is no me!!!

You all played a pivotal role in this series being birthed and I love you with my whole heart!!

The Game!!!

My heartaches every time I think of Shakita and Justice face

Who will never feel like Justice is served every time they think of their loved one on the curb

When I think of his siblings, they were always on go ready to fight for each other

When I think of Buck I cry because him and Shon was like shaq and kobe without 1 the game aint the same

When I think of my aunt who loss her son, my uncle who loss his son

My cousins who loss their brother, my spirit grieves because this was such an unnecessary, untimely death

But then I think about smiley with his million-dollar smile and I know he's at rest

To be absent from the body is to be present with the Lord

So, although we are suffering and grieving, I know he suffers no more

My prayer is that his soul made it in because you know us Martin's we love to fight and win

A mother loss her son, A WIFE LOSS HER HUSBAND, a daughter loss her father

But the game don't care about none of that so to everyone here today

I STRONGLY SAY PUT DOWN THE GUNS AND WALK AWAY

Men take your rightful positions and stand up

You can be forgiven for your past sins don't let anyone tell you different

1

Next time you ready to pull a trigger and take a life remember this pain you

Feel and know that it's not alright for you to take a life Jesus Loves you, you and you

No matter what you have done but now is the time for change cause yall cant keep

Leaving yall families behind to deal with this pain

We need our men yall are the foundation to the family dynamic

So stop bowing to this systemic slavery telling you this the only way

Rise up today because tomorrows not promised, and the kingdom of God has need of you

So, stay true and stop all this loyalty nonsense cause although you Love the game

The game don't love you

They say there are 2 ways out, death or jail but the devil is a liar because there is a 3rd way out

And his name is Jesus, who already paid the price for your life!

We feel pain, hurt and most of all anguish because my cousin said it

Best my grandma taught and raised a strong family but never taught us how to lose

Each other so today I proudly say our family will rise and God will give us beauty

For ashes but don't let your pride stop you because Jesus is the

Way the truth and life so don't get it twisted without him you won't win this fight!!!!

The Game part 2

When one enters the game it's not his intentions to change

But the reality is you can't remain the same

Everything from your perspective, to your intentions, to your character evolves

When you counting that money you not even thinking about problems being resolved

And you never counted the cost

Running from the cops, going to jail and being shot is normalized in our community

So right now I'm a take this opportunity to help push you along and change your mind

Cause when it comes to the game there is a thin line

Hate is the opposite of love but ironically love is the only thing that drives out hate

I can hear the door slamming on those cell gates, but we not enslaved to the man

We in bondage by our own hands

It's time for a new mentality, it's time to break free, break loose and untie the noose

When my cousin was murdered, I told my husband to pinch me and wake me up from this bad dream

But everything not always what it seems

I heard comments about his lifestyle, but sin is sin so if we being real none of us would make it in

It's only because Jesus paid the price that we can even have eternal life
So, before you judge examine yourself and see where you stand
It's time to put your life in our Heavenly Father's hands!

Part 3 (cycles)

The definition of insanity is doing the same thing over and over expecting different results

Do you remember how it felt when you had the devil on one shoulder pulling you this way

Angel on another saying there is a better way

Torn between the two and you just don't know what to do

Going insane so you decide to bury the pain

Generational cycles repeating themselves because we were never even taught how to ask for help

You want to do what's right but evil's always present

You pray Lord God just help me get into Heaven

Tired of seeing the cycle repeat itself so be the change you want to see in everyone else

The time we in is so crucial we got to stop doing what we use to

Let old things pass away, let's embrace the new, I don't want to lose anyone else to violence

I'm done being silenced

My voice will be heard, I don't mean to strike a nerve

It's time for new things, new life, new thoughts and everything right

I see your future so clearly and it can be bright

Let the darkness go it doesn't fit you well now let your light shine

You was created for greatness

Look at the man in the mirror, ask God to open your eyes so you can see clearer

That there's another way to provide so put your trust in the only 1 and true living God

You have the power to change, it's already inside you

You just have to confront the pain

Doing things your way has gotten you to the bar

Now let a higher power take over so you can go far

I'm talking beyond the stars, remove the limitations and watch God change your situation!

Part 4(Product of my Environment)

Environment is important to your growth so if you want to develop both

Peace and joy, then you must separate yourself from the noise

Grew up being exposed to so much, all you know is what you see

All you do is what you saw, which consisted of people running from the law

Parents running the streets and kids not always having enough to eat

So you made up in your mind that you would never go hungry or even be lonely

So the hood mentality caught you young and it's the only thing that rolls off your tongue

By design of the enemy your mind is confined

You get back what you put out so don't become a product of your environment

By getting sucked in the game but instead help the world change

Turn a negative into a positive

Choose to live, choose to forgive those that crossed you

Now boss up the right way and invest in bussin-esses

So you can stop running from badges

So you can get beauty for ashes

Next time your case gets tossed take it as a sign, come home

And don't get lost cause remember it cost

Thank the Lord for another day because in the game you never know
Who trying to get you out the way!

Part 5(Fake Friends)

Truth be told in the game you don't have no friends

You got to remember some sold their soul

You trying to figure out why you keep getting caught up thinking it's your enemy

But it's really the one with his feet up, because you made him so comfortable

When you living that life you have to think twice about the company you keep

Pay attention to their cheeks, whether it's a smile or a frown and watch who stay around

Nephew said "more people show up to your funeral than to your birthday because they rather see you on your back than on your feet" and that's the mentality you gotta have in these streets

See it's not worth it no peace, no joy, no time

You gotta watch your back cause of the snakes in the grass

The same ones who you would give your last

The wolves in sheeps clothing ready to attack soon as you let your guard down

Pay attention to the ones who don't stick around

When you down but when you up they show you fake love

These are fake friends

When you going to learn all their waiting on is their turn to take your spot closer to the top

Stop letting everybody in your circle the one next to you got the knife in your back

But you blind cause all you focused on is a check

But there is a real friend who will show you unconditional love and His

Name is Jesus and He sits above on the right hand of God

Who is the reason you are still alive!

Part 6(Expectations)

When you in the game everybody got their hand out

But when you in trouble they like iguanas not 1 stand out

When you need a helping hand how many people take a stand

To pull you up from the trenches, everyone sitting around chilling on the benches

But when the holidays come it's your job to provide for the family, the hood

Your friends and they wonder why you can't put this game to an end

Sometimes you wanna do what's right but expectations coming from left and right

And it's a fight but let me make this clear you are allowed to change your life

Especially for the better especially especially because you want to see your

Children grow up together

It's time for you to take a stand and get your life back

No more excuses the Lord will take you right back

Your life matters in more ways than you know so come on business man

And take this helping hand to put you on the right track

It's time to come up higher and you don't get there by being in the streets

The devil is a liar!

Part 7(Epidemic)

The man put the drugs on the streets and I know it's not fair
But we kept them there
Time for the addicts to be free because they got the right to live like you and me
I know I know if they don't get it from you, they will get it from someone else
But if everybody change, they gone have to deal with their health
There is plenty of wealth to go around now let me teach you a thing
Or two about how to really flip your life around
Take what you made and turn to the hills from which your help come
Ask God for wisdom in how to become who He created you to be
Cause life comes from him you see
Pumping poison into each other sowing seeds of disease and death
Tired of laying people to rest before their time
Just because of the desire to grind
Guns and drugs, drugs and guns in your heart you not even really a thug
You just need a tight hug so let me love on you real quick
And give you a real fix
The kind you never experienced from your parents
No disrespect to them cause they did the best they could
Most of us grew up in the same type of hood
Affection was frowned upon so you look to other people and things for love

Part of the reason the epidemic of drugs is so prevalent in our community

Not just drugs but the epidemic of hate EXIST

And it's up to us to create an epidemic of Love!

Part 8(Women Influence)

Ladies I love us but we gotta start using our power of influence for things that are just

God took us from man's rib because He knew they would need our help

It is Him who give us power to get wealth

As a help mate I ought to help get him to where he needs to be

That don't just help him it also helps me

Our roles are so important to the development of the man

But if your head in the sand, how can he stand

No we can't make choices for them or take accountability for their actions

But we can help guide them in the right directions

We were wonderfully and beautifully made in the image of God

So with Him we can be a guide to these men in the streets and

Cause the cease fires to increase

The movie chi-raq was crazy but they had the right idea

The power of women is so clear

We just have to readjust our focus, stop loving money more than our men

But we gotta learn to love our men more than sin

Love not gonna watch you on the road to destruction without speaking up

And at least trying to stop you

Ask yourself do you have his best interest at heart cause if you do try to convince

Him that it's time for a new start!

Part 9(Legacy)

The children affected by the game sometimes grow up being the same
As the parent who never taught them what change look like
Once you in that dirt all that lefts behind is your legacy
And hurt that your loved ones deal with
Now your children have to grow up without a father, did you even bother
To think of Babygirl and Babyboy when you decided the game would be your world
Some say they didn't choose the game, the game chose them
But the reality is we all have a choice to succumb
to our environment either you're the influencer or your being influenced
most of yall don't even know what yall doing
to the ones left to bury you when all your friends disappear only those who were true
will remain
when your gone you think your name will live on but that's only
temporarily cause once the phone stop ringing and the door stop knocking
all that's left is your family
what legacy do you wanna leave behind?
that your name ring bells in the street or that you found a better way for your family to eat
although your spirit lingers on, we know your gone

there is no coming back from death so decide your next steps
cause the devil don't know love that only comes from above
God is Love and Love is God so let him abide
in you from This day forward choose righteous over wrong choose
life over death
Choose peace over this mess!

Part 10(The End Game)

Now we've come to the end and the truth is it's not a game, so I'll say it again

It's time for change

Kids should be able to play in the streets kids should be able to grow up with

Their fathers being able to teach

Them in their homes, with no worries of being left alone so just stop and think

What you're leaving behind everyday when you leave out to grind

One day you may not return and then your child and your child's mom

Left with burdens they never asked for after you walked out the door

Families left with the expectations of raising your kids when they didn't ask for

That bid or lay down and have those kids

Love is Love and hate is hate, now let's open these prison gates

And be freed in our minds because we don't know how much time

We really have so let's make the time we do have last

Let's make it count now tell these streets you about to bounce

Matter fact don't announce it

move out in silence cause we all know

When you try to exit your life can hang in the balance

This game is such a challenge

Roe, Shon, Niesha, Rahdeen so many more that I can't even name

They never got the chance to change cause someone took their life

Don't let the devil control your mind learn to think for yourself

You can't turn back the hands of time

But you can decide what happens next you can decide to never go back

To life in the streets you can ask for forgiveness

And have a clean slate, a clean plate a new way to eat

Life is precious so choose not to take it for granted

Think of all the seeds you planted whether good or bad

Eventually they'll grow so don't be apart of the sad flow that's plaguing our community

But instead search for new opportunities

To turn it around you don't have to end up in the ground sooner than you need to

God has a purpose and a plan, He needs you!

PRAYER

Father, I humble myself before you giving you thanks for all that you want to do for our communities God, I thank you because all you need are willing vessels to bring about change in the earth, God I speak to the spirits of the women and call them to rise up Lord the wives the mothers the sisters the nieces the aunts the grandmothers the cousins to speak up about what we see and no longer condone the things that lead up to our men being taken from us give us the boldness to no longer be silent about the violence and no longer accepting it as " another day in the hood" convict the women as well as cause us to apply the pressure to get these men out the streets, but God, not just so they can live in positivity, but God so they can take their rightful positions in the Kingdom of God and have great success in you Lord God, I speak to the dry bones and I declare that they shall live ad not die God, I speak life to every dream and vision that you have given the people and I rebuke the spirit of fear, doubt and unbelief, the spirit of murder and the spirit of hate and I speak a right now change and overflow of your blessing in Jesus name I pray Amen!!!

www.ingramcontent.com/pod-product-compliance
Lightning Source LLC
Chambersburg PA
CBHW060358130626
46553CB00003B/1293